DENG LIANG

PIANO TECHNICAL EXERCISES

FOR

FINGERS INDEPENDENCE AND COORDINATION

Volume II

PARTRIDGE

Library of Congress Control Number: 2018912100
ISBN: Softcover 978-1-5437-7187-9
eBook 978-1-5437-7188-6

Because of the dynamic nature of the Internet, any web addresses or links contained in this book may have changed since publication and may no longer be valid. The views expressed in this work are solely those of the author and do not necessarily reflect the views of the publisher, and the publisher hereby disclaims any responsibility for them.

Print information available on the last page.

To order additional copies of this book, contact
Toll Free +65 3165 7531 (Singapore)
Toll Free +60 3 3099 4412 (Malaysia)
orders.singapore@partridgepublishing.com

www.partridgepublishing.com/singapore

Deng Liang
Southwest Minzu University
Chengdu, Sichuan, China

Proofreading: Shuangshuang Ma
Xueyao Dai
Shuyue Xu
Yiqiong Zhang
Ting Tang

Word count: ard. 200,100

Preface

The aim of these exercises is to train the independence and coordination of the fingers to allow the pianist to play the piano without any physical difficulties, especially with regard to the fingers' physical movements. The physiological restriction imposed on piano playing by the human hands is that the action of lifting the 2nd, 3rd, 4th, and 5th fingers is usually accomplished by the same extensor. This awkward phenomenon creates a physiological difficulty for piano playing. The 2nd finger has its own extensor; however, this only makes it more independent than the other fingers instead of making the other fingers' actions any easier. There are, of course, flexors and abductors, etc., which also affect the independence and coordination of different fingers. These exercises are carefully designed to train and conquer such physical restrictions. It should be noted that the exercises in this score are designed only for mechanical technical training and improvement of the finger movements and not for musicality.

All the exercises are based on the author's years of piano practice experiments and provide the optimum level of practice for refining the abilities of and coordination between fingers. Although some exercises are similar to other piano technical training studies, such as the exercises by Louis Plaidy, Camille-Marie Stamaty, Isidor Philipp Godowsky, Liszt and Brahms etc., and some of them are vaguely similar to some pianists' private finger exercises, this Volume II score by the author is a continuation of the Volume I, which is more comprehensive, systematic, detailed, complete and reliable for training the independence and coordination of each finger. To gain the utmost benefits from the logical progression of these exercises, it is recommended that these piano exercises be practiced on a daily basis and sequentially from the first to the last instead of in a random order. Through the focused and concentrated practice of these exercises, all piano students and players can attain the fundamentals of superb performance and play, especially with respect to the fingers' independent action.

For the manuscript notation in most of the exercises, the notes in brackets with the *fermata* indicate that the notes in the brackets should not be released during the exercise unless the player needs to play them; after being played, the notes should continue to be held.

The Volume II had actually been completed in Dec 1st, 2019. The publication was delayed due to the Covid-19 pandemic.

Caution: all the exercises in the Volume II need to be practiced in a reasonable way (methodology) in order to avoid unnecessary hand injuries.

Dr. Deng Liang

Southwest Minzu University

Chengdu, Sichuan, China

Sep 22nd, 2022.

PIANO TECHNICAL EXERCISES FOR FINGERS INDEPENDENCE AND COORDINATION

Volume II

(2019)

Deng Liang (1982-)

* The notes in the brackets should not be released during the exercise unless the player needs to play them; after being played, the notes should continue to be held.

3.
2
3
4
5
1 1
4.
2
3
4
5
1 1 1 1
5.
5
4
3
2
1 1
2
3
4
5
1 1

6.
7.
8.

9.
10.
11.

12.
13.
14.

15.
16.
17.

18.
5
4
2
1
19.
1
2
4
5
20.
1
2
4
5

21.
22.
23.

24.
25.
26.

27.
1
2
3
5
4 4
28.
1
2
3
5
4 4 4
29.
5
3
2
1
4 4
1
2
3
5
4 4

30.
31.
32.

33.
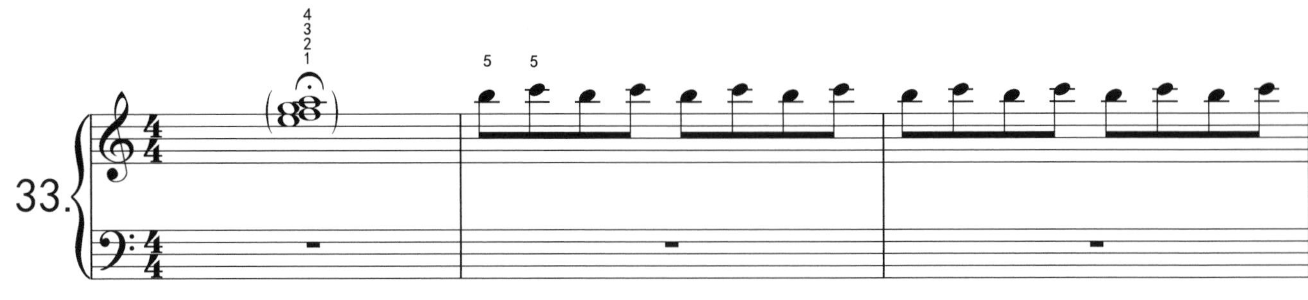

34.
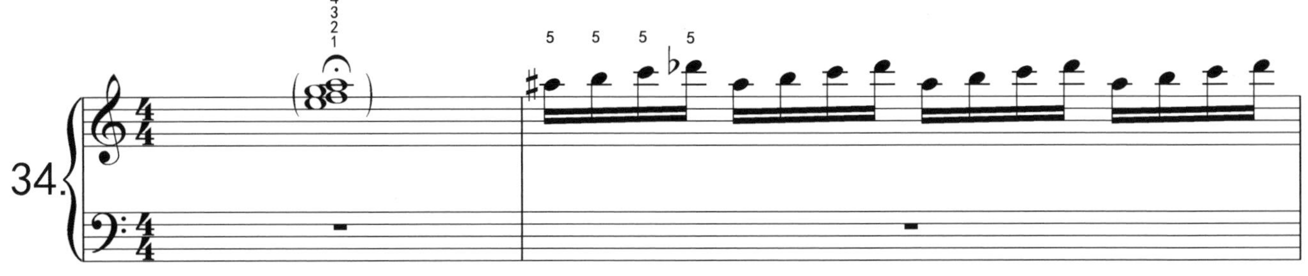

35.
36.
37.

38.
39.

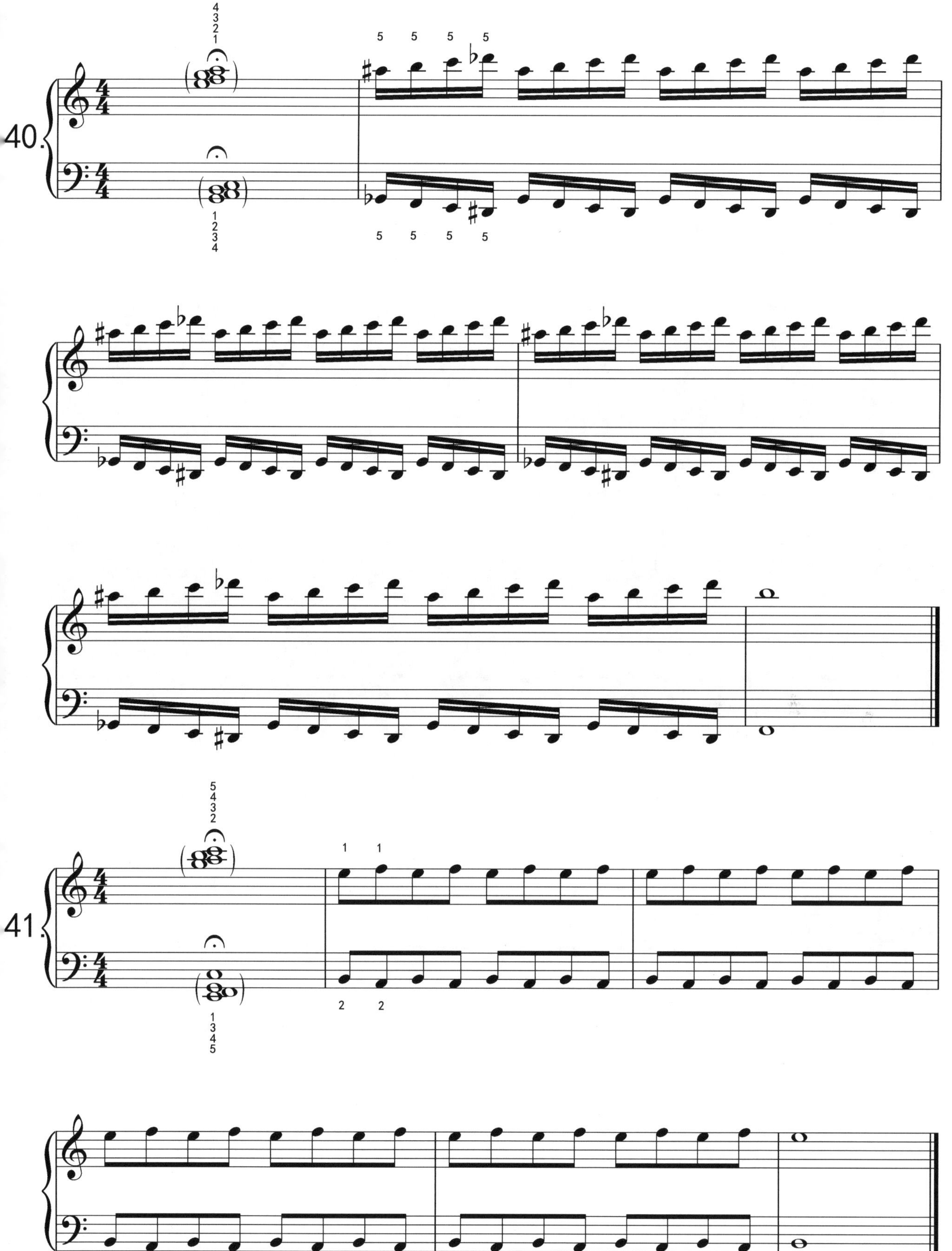
40.
41.

42.
43.
44.

45.
46.
47.

48.
49.
50.

51.
52.
53.

54.
55.
56.

57.

58.

59.

60.
61.
62.

63.
64.
65.

66.
67.
68.

69.
70.
71.

72.
73.
74.

75.
76.
77.

78.
79.
80.

81.

82.

83.

84.
85.
86.

87.
88.
89.

90.
91.
92.

93.
5
3
2
1
4 4
3 3
1
2
4
5
94.
5
3
2
1
4 4
3 3 3
1
2
4
5
95.
5
3
2
1
4 4
5 5
1
2
3
4

96.
97.
98.

99.
00.
01.

102.

103.

104.

05.
06.

107.
4 3 2 1
5 5
2 2
1 3 4 5
108.
4 3 2 1
5 5
3 3 3 3
2 2 2
1 3 4 5
109.
4 3 2 1
5 5
3 3
1 2 4 5

10.
11.
12.

113.
114.

15.
16.

117.
118.

19.
20.

121.
3
1
2
3
122.
2
1
3

23.
3
1
2
2
1
3
3
3

124.
125.

26.

127.
128.

29.

130.
131.

32.

133.
134.

35.

136.
137.

38.

139.

41.

142.
143.

44.

145.
146.

47.

148.

50.

151.

152.

53.

154.

155.

56.

157.

158.

59.

160.
161.

62.

163.

164.

65.

166.
167.

68.

169.
170.

71.

172.
173.

74.

175.
176.

77.

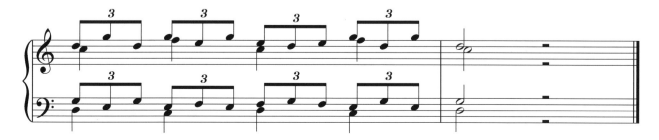

178.
179.

30.

181.
182.

83.

184.
185.

86.

187.

89.
4/4
4/4

190.
191.

92.

193.

194.

95.

196.
197.

98.

199.

01.

202.

203.

04.

205.
206.

07.

208.

209.

10.

211.
212.

3
3
13.
2
1
1
4

214.
215.

16.

217.

19.

220.

221.

22.

223.

224.

25.

226.

227.

28.

229.

230.

3
1
3
3
31.
3
1
4
3
3
3
3
3
3

232.

233.

34.

235.

236.

37.

238.

239.

40.

241.

242.

3
2
3
2
3
2
3
3
3

3
2
3
2
3
2
3
3
3

43.

5
2
1
4
3
4
3
4
3
3
3
3

4
3
4
3
4
3
3
3
3

4
3
4
3
4
3
3
3
3

4
3
4
3
4
3
3
3
3

244.
245.

1
2
1
2
1
2
3
3
3
1
2
1
2
1
2
3
3
3
46.
1
4
5
2
3
2
3
2
3
3
3
3
2
3
2
3
2
3
3
3
3
2
3
2
3
2
3
3
3
3
2
3
2
3
2
3
3
3
3

247.

248.

49.

250.
251.

52.

253.
254.

55.

2
3
2
3
2
3
3
3
3
5
2
3
2
3
2
3
3
3
3
1
3
4
3
4
3
4
3
3
3
2
3
4
3
4
3
4
3
3
3
3
4
3
4
3
4
3
3
3
5
3
4
3
4
3
4
3
3
3

256.

Printed in the United States
by Baker & Taylor Publisher Services